A TALENT FOR DETAIL

A TALENT FOR DETAIL

The Photographs of

MISS FRANCES BENJAMIN JOHNSTON

1889-1910

BY PETE DANIEL AND RAYMOND SMOCK

HARMONY BOOKS

Publisher: Bruce Harris
Editor: Linda Sunshine
Production: Gene Connor, Murray Schwartz and Frank Colosa
Book Design: Shari de Miskey and Linda Sunshine
A TALENT FOR DETAIL was printed in duotone, a two color process by
Publishers Production International on 70 lb. Meade Matte. The
text was set in 12 pt. Bodoni Book, display heads in filmset.

Acknowledgments

We are especially indebted to the staff of the Prints and Photographs
Division of the Library of Congress for their invaluable
professionalism. Milton Kaplan was especially helpful with
suggestions and encouragement, as were Virginia Daiker, Jerald
C. Maddox, Jerry Kearns, and Leroy Bellamy. Carolyn Sung of the
Manuscript Division of the Library of Congress aided us in our
search of the Johnston Papers. The University of Illinois Press offered
original encouragement and sponsored collection of the photographs
for this volume. Louis R. Harlan first introduced us to Johnston's
photographs and lent us his notes on the Ramer incident. The
following people gave support at various stages of development:
Sam Boone, Ralph Bourne, Dennis Burton, Barbara Kraft,
Sharyn Mitchell, Donald Ritchie, Marvin Sadik, and Anne Tucker.

All photographs and other illustrations in this volume are from
the Prints and Photographs Division of the Library of Congress,
Washington, D. C.

A photo-essay by the authors, "Frances Benjamin Johnston's
American Album," appeared in the Spring 1973 issue of The
Maryland Historian.

We would also like to thank Mrs. Alice Roosevelt Longworth who was
kind enough to view Johnston's photographs and comment on the ones
she particularly remembered. In 1902 Mrs. Longworth met and was
photographed by Frances Benjamin Johnston. We have included
Mrs. Longworth's comments in the book as additional captions to the
photographs.

For
Stella Hunt Daniel and the memory of
Peter Edward Daniel
and
Richard and Helen Smock

Contents

A PHOTOBIOGRAPHY

2

A PHOTOBIOGRAPHY

In 1897 Frances Benjamin Johnston wrote an article for the *Ladies Home Journal* entitled "What a Woman Can Do with a Camera," advising women how to become photographers. Probably revealing her self-concept more than offering advice, she stated, "The woman who makes photography profitable must have, as to personal qualities, good common sense, unlimited patience to carry her through endless failures, equally unlimited tact, good taste, a quick eye, a talent for detail, and a genius for hard work." Johnston personified all these qualities, but "a talent for detail" became her trademark.

Johnston's sharp eye often transformed photographs into symbolic documents. Many of her group poses can actually be cropped into a number of perfectly composed smaller studies. Her spectrum of photographic work was enormous—rich and poor, black and white, men and women, famous and obscure, young and old—and whether recording proud workers, famous Americans, or scenic splendor, she composed a portrait that evoked a

Third from left, second row: Frances Johnston as an art student

true and lasting visual suggestion of the age. The works published here represent her ambitious attempt to visually capture two decades of the American scene, and these photographs of the 1890s and the first decade of the twentieth century are a rich legacy, a mosaic of the era.

Her career, however, did not end in 1910. By then she was internationally recognized as one of America's leading documentary, portrait, and artistic photographers. She began to specialize in garden photography and concluded her long career as an architectural photographer in the 1930s. Throughout some fifty years as a working photographer, she continually set her own standards and followed her own intuition. In 1900 a critic summed up Johnston's individuality, noting that her photography "is of no particular school or class. She follows no traditions and no rules."

Born in Grafton, West Virginia, on 15 January 1864, Frances Benjamin Johnston spent her early years along the Ohio River, in Rochester, New York, and in Washington, D.C. She studied art at Notre Dame Convent in Govanston, Maryland, and in 1883 began a two year study at the Académie Julien in Paris. When she returned to Washington, D.C., after studying art abroad, she enrolled at the Art Student's League (which was later incorporated in the Corcoran Gallery School), but she had lost her enthusiasm for American art. Aided by a journalist friend, she began making illustrations for a newspaper and then, sensing the changing trend in illustrated journals, turned to photography because she thought it was "the more accurate medium."

Johnston was among the early illustrators to realize the significant role that photography could play in journalism. According to tradition, she asked George Eastman to recommend a camera suitable for press photography. Eastman, founder of the Eastman Kodak Company, had only recently marketed his first Kodak, and he sent Johnston one with his compliments. She studied photography formally under the direction of Thomas William Smillie, then in charge of the Division of Photography of the Smithsonian Institution in Washington, and she bravely launched her own career.

In the 1890s Johnston was known as the "photographer of the American Court." She did a series on the White House, on homes of top administration leaders, and on foreign legations. These photographs record a large segment of official Washington in the 1890s. Foreshadowing her later career

5

as an architectural photographer, the White House photographs were published as a book, *The White House,* in 1893. Frances Johnston was distantly related to Mrs. Grover Cleveland, and whether it was family ties or her characteristic persistence that opened the doors of official Washington, she stalked American leaders for the next fifteen years, leaving behind an incredible documentary record.

Hers was a documentary eye, often focused on the mundane, as if Johnston knew that one day others would look at her photographs to recapture the period in which she worked. Documentary photography was well under way even before Frances Johnston was born, of course, but by the 1890s the camera, thanks to George Eastman, was getting into the hands of ordinary citizens for the first time on a large scale. Interest in photography of almost any subject was high. Johnston's engaging personality, boldness, and photographic talent were the perfect formula to guarantee her success in press photography.

Though she never won the critical acclaim of Alfred Stieglitz or other artistic photographers of her day, she did concentrate on photography as an art form. In 1898, the year she exhibited at the New York Camera Club, she sent some prints to Stieglitz, and he wrote to her that "your work is capital, & I shall be glad to see more of it when you get to New York." That she thought in artistic terms often comes through in her observations. "It is wrong to regard photography as purely mechanical." (It was mechanical up to a point, she conceded.) "In portraiture, especially, there are so many possibilities for picturesque effects—involving composition, light and shade, the study of pose, and arrangement of drapery—that one should go for inspiration to such masters as Rembrandt, Van Dyck, Sir Joshua Reynolds, Romney and Gainsborough, rather than to compilers of chemical formulae."

Her contribution to photography was not in technology or in artistic innovation but in excellence as a practitioner of her art. "I wore out one camera after another," she bragged, "and I never had any of those fancy gadgets. Always judged exposure by guess." Once a technique worked she often stuck with it, perhaps at a sacrifice to experimentation. She used the developing agent Eikonogen, for example, long after most photographers had abandoned it as obsolete. Perhaps her genius was in doing the ordinary exceptionally well.

Center: Frances Johnston selling tintypes at a Virginia county fair in May 1903

The Green Room, redecorated in 1893

The Green Room at the White House in 1890

Wives of Cleveland's Cabinet, photographed in Johnston's Washington studio on 4 January 1897. *Left to right:* Olive Harmon, Jane P. Francis, M. J. Carlisle, Agnes P. Olney, Frances Cleveland, Nannie H. Wilson, Juliet K. Lamont, Leila Herbert

Clockwise from bottom left: F. B. Johnston, F. Holland Day, Clarence H. White, Gertrude Käsebier, Henry Troth, 1899

Though Johnston did mostly documentary and portrait photography in the 1890s, she earned a reputation as an artistic photographer, one of the vanguard. No better example of this can be found than the fact that she was chosen a member of the jury for the 1899 Philadelphia Photographic Society exhibit. The Philadelphia show a year earlier had pointed a new direction in photographic standards, a concentration on the "artistic quality of the photograph." Alfred Stieglitz had been on the jury in 1898, and the show was significant because it "was the first exhibition of photography in America to take place with the active sponsorship of a recognized fine arts institution." Stieglitz sat on a jury composed of another photographer and three painters. Significantly, the 1899 jury that included Johnston was composed of the five photographers shown in the accompanying tintype.

Gertrude Käsebier of New York specialized in portraits and, like Johnston, did work for magazines. She later joined the Photo-Secession, a group of photographers in America founded by Alfred Stieglitz and others, who promoted the idea that photography was a fine art, comparable to painting and other arts. F. Holland Day was an amateur, recognized both in the United States and in Europe as an excellent artistic photographer. Clarence H. White, who still kept his grocers' job in Newark,

11

Ohio, had been discovered by Stieglitz and also played a founding role in the Photo-Secession movement. Henry Troth was an amateur from Philadelphia and had a one man show at the Camera Club of New York in 1897.

As Jerald C. Maddox of the Prints and Photographs Division of the Library of Congress recently pointed out, the 1899 jury was "the first all photographer jury to judge a major photographic exhibition. This was a revolutionary step that not only suggested that photographers might be esthetically sensitive, but also implied that in this respect they might be the equals of artists in the traditional media."

Two years later only Johnston was left to represent the artistic photographers as a juror at the Philadelphia show, and in that year the salon lost its prominence. In 1902 the Photo-Secession movement was launched in America with a counterpart in Europe called the Linked Ring. Alfred Stieglitz was the international head of the movement. Believing wholeheartedly in the main goal of encouraging recognition of photography as an art form and in the concept that the photograph could be as intimate and revealing as a painting,

Frances Johnston became an associate member of the Photo-Secession in 1904.

Johnston's huge photograph collection in the Library of Congress is still being processed, and part of it remains in unsorted condition in the original file cabinets. Despite the fact that the Manuscript Division of the Library of Congress has some 17,000 items of her correspondence, these documents reveal far less than might be expected. She was a fiercely independent person who often scoffed at social conventions; yet her private life remains hidden behind a veil of Victorian manners. Her letters speak lightly of the weather, of travel, and other polite topics that frustrate the biographer. More often her surviving correspondence concerns business details or notes she made to herself regarding her work. She might, for example, make a notebook entry that explained the coloration of a garden scene so that she could make a hand-colored print at a later time. Her papers reveal that she was absorbed by her photography and often did not give proper attention to business matters, sometimes even failing to open bills. Often, when the excitement of a new assignment was over, she failed to rush her prints on to the

Johnston working in the basement of her Washington studio, July 1895

13

Motoring, 1904 style

Wading at La Ciobat, France, 1905

market and let business suffer while she searched for new friends and adventure. Her agent, George Grantham Bain, expressed his frustration with her in an 1899 letter. "You have caused me serious losses by not delivering promptly prints of pictures which I knew had been taken."

Her friends referred to Frances as a small, frail, but very attractive woman. Photographs reveal little of the fragility but rather capture her dynamism and strength. More than anything, she detested inactivity, and she drew others into her orbit as she moved from America to frequent vacations in Europe. In 1899 a man she met on a European tour wrote that the "trip to Pompeii was thoroughly enjoyed by me and there is no doubt in my mind that I could not have had a more agreeable companion, and my only regret is that the time was so short." Another friend who traveled with Frances noted that she was always up early, making calls and keeping appointments, returning only for her evening bourbon and dinner. An American admirer wrote to her in 1902 saying she was "one of the genuine people, of whom there are too few in the world. We like your stories, Frances, but we like you even better."

Johnston never married, but devoted her life to photography. Any love affairs she may have had are not revealed in her correspondence. How she felt on social issues or other topics is seldom discussed except as it relates to her work. Her most revealing written work, not surprisingly, is the writing that describes her photography. Anyone who goes through her letters and then her photographs will be struck by the richness of her photographic record. The single best source to study her life is her photographs. While she was documenting the American scene, she was also recording her own life. Her camera was her diary. From self-portraits, snapshots taken by others, and photographs of her studio and friends, one can at least glimpse a slice of Bohemian life.

In the early 1890s Frances built a studio in the rose garden behind her father's Washington house. Before the studio was built she had developed her plates in the bathroom of her parents' home. In the new studio she did most of her portrait work, developed negatives, printed photographs, and conducted her business.

But her extraordinary studio was also the meeting place of her friends. She hid the camera and apparatus, and the studio became intimate—a fireplace, piano, couches, chairs—a place of good cheer. Every Wednesday afternoon would be devoted to her friends who gathered at the studio. Her crowd was called "The Push." Surprisingly, her correspondence contains little that illuminates these friends and their relationship to her. However, according to available information, these men and women were a segment of the artistic community of Washington, with old family friends and even her mother, whom Frances called "Muddie," and Aunt Nin included at times. Those who did write to her would occasionally mention roasting corn or apples, or singing, or just sitting around talking and drinking wine. A better description of this set can be seen in photographs; Johnston was the centrice.

Johnston really lived two lives during the 1890s. She was a properly conventional Victorian woman who had entry to the White House and the circles of official Washington. But, on the other hand, her friends and associates were artists, poets, playwrights, and actors whose lifestyles often mocked the Victorian conventions that Johnston publicly upheld. She apparently moved with ease between these two worlds. To the eyes of some of her contemporaries the very fact that she was a woman in a male-dominated profession marked her as an unconventional person.

The studio, behind 1332 V Street N.W., about 1895

A twelve-by-sixteen-foot skylight dominated one side of the studio. "I have tried to make my skylight room as artistic, as cheerful and as inviting as would be the studio of an artist," Johnston explained.

Wall opposite the skylight

The Push
"Frances is our hostess, Frances is our joy.
She gives us many a party, likewise many a toy.
So here's to Frances' great success, with coal and bread
    and butter
Long may she wave and entertain, and often snap the
    shutter."

Entertaining friends before the studio fireplace, about 1895

21

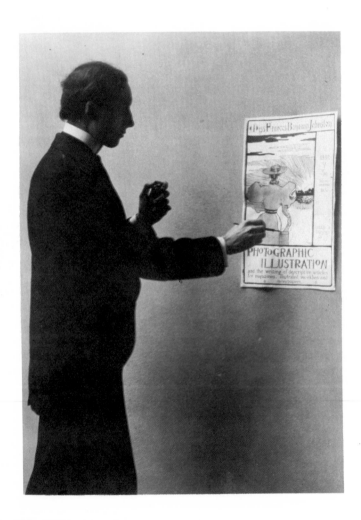

Mills Thompson was probably a regular visitor at the studio, though in 1896 he left Washington and "The Push" for a position in the Bohemian Studio in New York. He was remembered for "ventriloquism, his inimitable songs, his clever imitations, his droll dancing." He was also good with the brush and pencil, as shown by the poster he did for Frances. The *Washington Post* gossip column noted that prior to departure "he is to decorate a set of tin furnace pipes which at present disfigure the studio of a young woman here,"—obviously Frances Johnston's. Whether it was on this last sentimental visit or sometime earlier, Johnston managed to record him in some of his "clever imitations."

23

Photographs of Mills Thompson by Frances Johnston

Posing with her mother in San Francisco, October 1903

Despite the Bohemian aspect of Johnston's life, she was neither a crusader nor a reformer. Her work does, however, show a comprehensive interest in and concern for humanity, especially for the role of women in American life. Women appear in many of Johnston's portraits, and she documented many women's activities ranging from the laying of the cornerstone of Memorial Continental Hall to the cloistered halls of a convent. Because photography meant so much to her creative life, she also encouraged other women to find self-expression through the lens.

Many of her contemporary women photographers were exclusively portraitists or specialists in photographs of children, dogs, or cats. These were demanding fields, to be sure, but areas where women could work with ease without raising eyebrows. There were many other women in photography at the turn of the century such as Lillian Baynes Griffin, Jessie Tarbox Beals, Edith H. Tracy, and, of course, Gertrude Käsebier. Lillian Griffin, who had to ask the dealer how to use her first camera, began in 1908 and became a prize-winning photographer of famous people. Jessie Tarbox Beals, a Massachusetts school teacher, began with a camera that cost her $1.75. She specialized in photo-journalism. Beals used her camera as a tool for social reform much as Jacob Riis had done, working for tenement reform and for prevention of cruelty to animals. Many women, as well as men, who earned modest reputations with their cameras in the 1890s, took up the craft as a hobby. Edith Tracy said she began photography "as an amusement" but found that she could profitably sell her work.

Johnston, however, took up photography as a business; it was no idle amusement for her. "I have not been able to lose sight of the pecuniary side," she emphasized, "though for the sake of money or anything else I would never publish a photograph which fell below the standard I have set for myself."

After 1910 Frances Benjamin Johnston began to drift away from photo-journalism and portrait work and entered more and more into garden and architectural photography. From 1913 to 1917 she and a friend, Mattie Edwards Hewitt, ran a studio on Fifth Avenue in New York. They obtained a contract to photograph the New Theater in New York which led to other successes. They did work for a long list of architects, businesses, and estates, including Carrere & Hastings; McKim, Mead &

At the Georgetown Convent of the Order of Visitation Nuns in 1900

On 19 April 1903 Johnston, herself a member of the Daughters of the American Revolution (though her paternal great-great-grandfather fought for the British), was on hand to document the laying of the cornerstone of the Memorial Continental Hall in Washington, D.C.

The proper Victorian

Three symbols of rebellion against Victorian formality appear in this self-portrait taken about 1896. Proper Victorian women were not expected to smoke, to drink beer, or to reveal their petticoats.

White; City National Bank; the North German Lloyd Co.; and the estates of John Pierpont Morgan, John J. Astor, and Mrs. Harry Payne Whitney.

By 1920 Johnston had become a sought-after lecturer on gardens, beginning another major phase of her career. She wrote in that year that she was beginning a tour from Cleveland through the Middle West into California. "My lectures appeal not only to garden clubs, but also to organizations fostering civic improvement, art and literary study, in that I endeavor to present the best sources of information on a wide range of subjects relating to gardens and flowers." By this time she had delved into color photography and was probably the first woman photographer to specialize in color processing. In 1930 she collaborated with Henry Irving Brock in *Colonial Churches in Virginia.*

In the 1930s she began the final phase of her career, winning a $26,000 Carnegie grant to photograph colonial southern architecture. In her late sixties at the time, she was reputed to have "the energy of a 20-year-old." She went about the South in a chauffeur-driven automobile locating old buildings, and it was said that she could "smell out an old colonial house five miles off the highway." Her mission was not to photograph the prominent homes of colonial America which, she argued, had already "been photographed often and well." Rather, she sought "the old farm houses, the mills, the log cabins of the pioneers, the country stores, the taverns and inns, in short those buildings that had to do with the everyday life of the colonists." She did her work well, and two books resulted from this venture, *The Early Architecture of North Carolina* and *The Early Architecture of Georgia.* In 1945 she was awarded an honorary membership in the American Institute of Architects.

Johnston moved to New Orleans in 1940 and entered a life of semi-retirement. Always independent, she lived a rather lonely life in her last years, but her energy did not subside. She bought a run-down house on the "respectable" end of Bourbon Street and transformed its dilapidated courtyard into a beautiful garden with a small pool. Continuing to pursue her interests in gardening, she often went out in her old Buick to give lectures. Her active days in the darkroom were over, even though she maintained a photographic work area in an alcove off her bathroom.

Age was slowing her down. She walked with a cane, and her doctor weaned her from bourbon; so she drank cherry wine instead. Even at this

Frances B. Johnston in 1936

33

stage of her life she remained staunchly indomitable. "I've learned not to depend on the Lord. I'll make the changes myself." She loved to roam the French Quarter and sit in bars and talk. Once when someone recognized her as a famous photographer, she agreed, "Yes, I'm the greatest woman photographer in the world."

In 1947, when she donated her prints, negatives, and correspondence to the Library of Congress, she returned to Washington in triumph as the Library held an exhibit of her work, bringing her some welcomed attention in her old age. The Library staff still remembers her as an outspoken woman in a floppy hat, still entertaining, engaging, a "character." She returned to New Orleans and died there on 16 March 1952.

The courtyard of her New Orleans home in the 1940s

Frances Benjamin Johnston with Librarian of Congress Luther H. Evans, examining some of Johnston's architectural photographs, 1947

FRANCES-B-JOHNSTON

An 1898 caricature by Felix Malony

THE DOCUMENTARY EYE

Stacks of money at the United States Bureau of Printing and Engraving, 1890

AMERICA AT WORK

Uncle Sam's Money

Frances Benjamin Johnston's photographic career began in December 1889 when *Demorest's Family Magazine* published the first of a two-part series on the United States Mint in Philadelphia and the Bureau of Engraving and Printing in Washington. Epitomizing the evolving nature of journal illustrations, only two photographs were published in the series, and as routine as they were, these photographs portended her career. One was an architectural shot of the facade of the U.S. Mint, and the other was a portrait of the director of the Mint. The other illustrations were engravings copied from her photographs. In these articles, as in others done in the 1890s for *Demorest's*, Johnston exhibited a marked writing ability; her prose was clear, informative, chatty. Yet, when she became a more successful photographer in the mid-1890s, she seldom supplied the text for her photographs.

man, provided with clumsy-looking gloves, grasps a strip of metal, thrusts the pointed end underneath the press, and presto! a dozen disks, or "blanks," neatly cut, fall into the tray beneath. While the work has been comparatively exact, and every disk among the thousands sent from the Rolling Room will weigh within a half-dozen grains of the standard weight, still the law requires that every coin must come within one and a half grains of the legal rate. Thus, before fit for coinage, every blank must be weighed and adjusted. As they come from the Rolling Room they are

WHITENING PROCESS.

bits of dingy metal, still greasy and dirty, and together with the strips from which they have been cut are sent to the cellar to be washed with soap and water. Cleansed and dried, the blanks go to the Adjusting Room, while the clippings are turned over to the Melter and Refiner, to be remelted and again cast into ingots.

The Adjusting Room, furnished with a dozen long tables and innumerable tiny scales, is where women find employment in the Mint. Here the blanks come from their cleaning, and are turned over to the forewoman of the room. From her they go in lots to the women who sit at the long tables, each with a pair of delicate scales before her, a file within reach, and a series

DESTRUCTION OF THE DIES.

of quaintly shaped metal boxes ranged about. The standard weight of a silver dollar blank is 412½ grains, with a legal tolerance of one and a half grains, more or less. Therefore the work here is to select the blanks of proper weight, file down the "heavies" and sort out the "lights," for a second test by that most ingenious machine the "Automatic Adjuster." Each class of blanks has a series of metal boxes, of a shape peculiar to itself, so that the shape

of the box determines at once the character of the blanks it contains, and there is no danger of mixing them after the adjustment of the weight.

In the Adjusting Room the noise of the machine-shops has been left behind, and the work goes on quickly and effectively amid the subdued rattle of the blanks, the click of the neat balances, the rasping of the deftly handled files, and the hum of scores of feminine tongues. Seemingly, their fingers move by instinct; and to what purpose it will be understood when it is stated that the present force handles $80,000 daily, averaging 120,000 blanks, each blank being separately adjusted.

Having been "weighed in the balance," the blanks are sent down to the Coining Room. The Automatic Adjuster takes them up, and with mechanical impartiality weighs each one fed into the receiving tubes, but drops the "standards" directly down, and slips the "heavies" to one side, and the "lights" to the other. The "lights" thus found wanting are again melted down; while the "standards" and "heavies" are put through the process known as "milling." This consists

of turning up the edge of the metal disk, and is a neat method, dating back many centuries, of preventing acquisitive people from clipping the edges of coins, and thus levying tribute on every one passing through their grasping fingers. The milling machines are rapid workers, and will operate on over five hundred half-dime planchets per minute, with an average of more than one hundred per minute of the larger silver coins.

Adjusted and milled, the blanks, which are now termed "planchets,"

COINING PRESS.

are ready for the impress from the die; but they are still dingy bits of metal, and must therefore be whitened, or blanched. For this purpose they are sent to the Whitening Room, where the furniture consists of an annealing furnace, some big troughs of water, and a noisily revolving crib, or hopper. The planchets are put into the furnace, heated cherry-red, plunged into a bath of dilute sulphuric acid, rinsed, and dumped into the hopper with sawdust, to dry. They come from the press a beautiful, gleaming white, and all that remains to make them money, is the stamp of the coining press.

The invention of a Frenchman, M. Thoumelier, the Steam Coining Press was introduced into the Mint in 1836, and, after undergoing many changes and improvements, stands, to-day, a model of perfection and ingenuity. The mechanism is simple, the obverse die being set in a brass plate, or triangle, set with a ball-and-socket joint upon the heavy metal arm which works through the massive iron arch

For their illustrations, newspapers and magazines in the 1880s relied heavily on zinc engravings, which were relatively easy for an artist to make from a drawing or photograph. The halftone process was known in 1850 but did not appear until 1880 in the *New York Daily Graphic*. In the 1890s the use of zinc engravings declined as a visual medium and they were often mixed with photographs in the same illustrated article. In January 1904 the *London Daily Mirror* became the first daily newspaper in the world to use photography exclusively for its illustrations.

The three pictures at left show how *Demorest's Family Magazine* reproduced Johnston's photographs as line engravings.

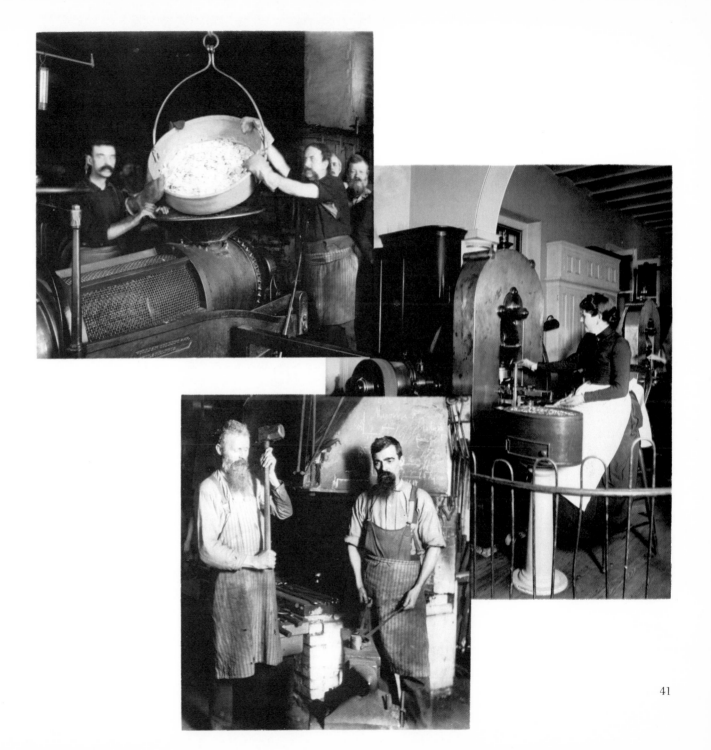

41

Through the Coal Country with a Camera

In 1891 Frances Johnston traveled to Shenandoah City, Pennsylvania, to photograph the Kohinoor Mines. The idea came from W. Jennings Demorest, publisher of *Demorest's Family Magazine*. He wrote on 21 June 1891, hesitantly asking for the article. He warned of the danger of explosion from the use of the magnesium powder flash which would be necessary for photographing in the mines. The technique had been used before, however; so Demorest believed Johnston could do it.

Johnston descended into a mine "where there would be the least possible risk, and no danger of igniting gas or fire-damp by the explosion of the magnesium powder." It took her four hours "of very hard work" to get three negatives, and although the photographs were flat, she deemed them "more than usually successful." She also commented on the problems of underground photography. Any underground subject was difficult, she explained, but in a coal mine the problems "were almost overwhelming, as everything was so hopelessly black, excepting the blank white reflections caught on the polished surfaces of the coal, while the atmosphere was fogged and heavy with dampness, smoke, and a fine, gritty dust."

But her interest went beyond the interior of the mine. She mixed with the workers, talked to them, and then visited their homes where she was "constantly offered a hospitality, were it but a cup of tea or a bite of lunch, so spontaneous, simplehearted, and kindly, that it was a delight to accept it." The entire area was covered with coal dust. "As a matter of course," she explained, "everything and everybody is black. Great, unsightly frame buildings—the coal breakers—dingy with dirt and culm, while the small cottages and rude wooden shanties of the miners cluster drearily about the outskirts." But the people who lived there had a dignity that impressed Frances. Characteristically, she moved easily among the people, winning their favor. "The people everywhere claimed my interest, which was returned in a measure, as everybody seemed to have a personal concern in the success of my pictures, and were always ready to pose with the utmost patience." She ended her article on a note of nostalgia. "I confess to the strange charm of the people, their labor, and the country. I would like to go back some day. I shall be very sorry if I don't."

Breaker Boys At Kohinoor Mines. When Johnston visited the breakers, chutes used to divide the coal from the slate, she observed "bright-eyed youngsters" and noted that "it must be a specially agile bit of slate that can escape their keen vision and nimble fingers."

Men and machines scrape the earth of its iron wealth at the Mesabi Range in 1903.

The Iron Men

In the 1850s iron ore mining operations began along northern Lake Superior, and by the time Johnston arrived in 1903 to record the scene with her camera, the range was producing one-sixth of the world's iron ore. Instead of descending into the earth to mine the ore, men could scoop up ore by the ton in steam shovels, haul it by train to the docks at Duluth or Superior, and ship it to the furnaces further south. The Mesabi Range, the heart of the mining operation, was sixty miles from the northern shore of Lake Superior and the ore, some 13 million tons a year, was taken from the area. An observer could see giant steam shovels strip away the ore; a five-ton shovel could load fifty tons on a car in three minutes and load a ten car switching train in thirty minutes. When railroad magnate James J. Hill visited the mines, he observed that the "problem of ore-production is principally a problem of the proper switching of trains."

Johnston managed to capture the magnitude of the mining operation; men eclipsed by giant machinery, the earth ripped open, smoke, dust, mammoth ore docks and ships. Her camera did not have a wide enough lens to capture it all, but nevertheless, one sees the essence of the mining operation in her study. Johnston had taken pity on the earth when she visited the Pennsylvania coal mines in 1892, and she must have pondered what was happening environmentally in Minnesota. When the miners came they removed the trees, then the thin layer of soil, and finally the giant shovels began to tear into the earth, digging themselves into a pit until the ore was exhausted. It was not a pretty sight, but it made men wealthy and thrust the United States into world leadership in the steel industry.

Ore dock worker, 1903

A miner, 1903

The tugboat *Joe Harris*

Loading iron ore

Women Workers

In a Lynn, Massachusetts, shoe factory in 1895, Johnston not only took this series of photographs but, characteristically, took time to visit the homes of the women and discuss their wages and working conditions. She found the same kind of dignity among the women in Lynn that she had found among the miners in Pennsylvania. Though the slower workers could earn only three to five dollars per week for their labor, she observed that they lived comfortably.

52

53

In 1910 Frances Johnston photographed women working in a cigar-box factory

NATIONAL HEROES

Get Dewey, Dewey, Dewey!

In the early summer of 1899 Frances Johnston decided it was time for a European vacation. She had some commissions in Paris to keep her busy there. But just before she sailed, she mentioned her trip to George Grantham Bain, her agent, and he suggested that as long as she was going she might take some photographs of Admiral George Dewey, who was making several stops at European ports before returning to the United States. There had been few photographs of Dewey or his ships since his victory at Manila Bay the year before.

The question, of course, was how does a woman get aboard a battleship. Johnston solved this problem by appealing to a man who was very responsible for Dewey's success at Manila, Theodore Roosevelt. Roosevelt, then assistant secretary of the Navy, had sent instructions to Dewey to prepare the fleet for battle before hostilities with Spain had begun. When the war broke out, Dewey was able to steam directly into Manila Bay and wreck the Spanish fleet. Johnston tracked Roosevelt to Oyster Bay, presented her card, and he hastily scribbled a note across it. "My dear Admiral

Dewey, Miss Johnston is a lady, and whom I personally know. I can vouch for, she does good work, and any promise she makes she will keep."

Bain then gave her special instructions. "Get Dewey, Dewey, Dewey! Get him walking, riding, eating and drinking. Then get views of the *Olympia* from every quarter." Bain's list of what to get went on for a paragraph. But he was also a bit worried about a photographer named J. C. Hemment who was off to do the same assignment. Bain had always found Hemment reliable, but he noted that "two or three persons have said to me lately that he was tricky, so it will be as well to be on your guard."

Johnston took George Bain at his word. She arrived in Naples at night, went immediately to the *Olympia*, presented her card, won approval, and showed up the next morning ready for work. She took some 150 photographs, and as Bain had suggested, she covered the ship. From time to time she would go to the torpedo room to reload her plate holders. Evidently she made a hit with Dewey and the crew of the ship. They "opened up" for her, and she managed to get her usual excellent photographs. While on board the *Olympia*, Frances filled out an enlistment record. Her trade was listed as

"Snapshots," and she rated a 5 (excellent) in everything from Seamanship to Marksmanship, except for Sobriety in which she rated a 4.9.

At that point the destiny of the photographs became a mystery. They were probably taken on 5 August, and by the eleventh Bain was already complaining that the Dewey market was "slipping away from us." Other photographers had also managed to capture Dewey. On 25 August Bain was in a panic. J. C. Hemment had returned with his photographs and was hawking them all over the country, but Bain had not even heard from Johnston though he had given her his cable address and had urged her to cable him how many photographs she had taken and when they would arrive. "And WHY did you entrust your negatives to the only person who was working against you?" Bain wrote in desperation. "Of course I have not got them yet." Finally on 2 September a small parcel arrived.

Evidently Hemment had charmed Frances, taken her negatives, and conveniently left them in London. His photographs beat hers by nine days though both were developed in Naples at the same time. Johnston never revealed exactly what happened in Naples, why she trusted Hemment, why the negatives were so tardy; perhaps she thought, in

Victorian terms, that a gentleman could be trusted in his dealings with a lady. But a more likely explanation is that she was anxious to begin her tour, anxious to be rid of the responsibility of the prints. Fortunately her photographs were good enough to sell quite well despite being late on the market.

Admiral George Dewey examines Johnston's work aboard the battleship *Olympia*.

Admiral Dewey at his desk

The Admiral's quarters

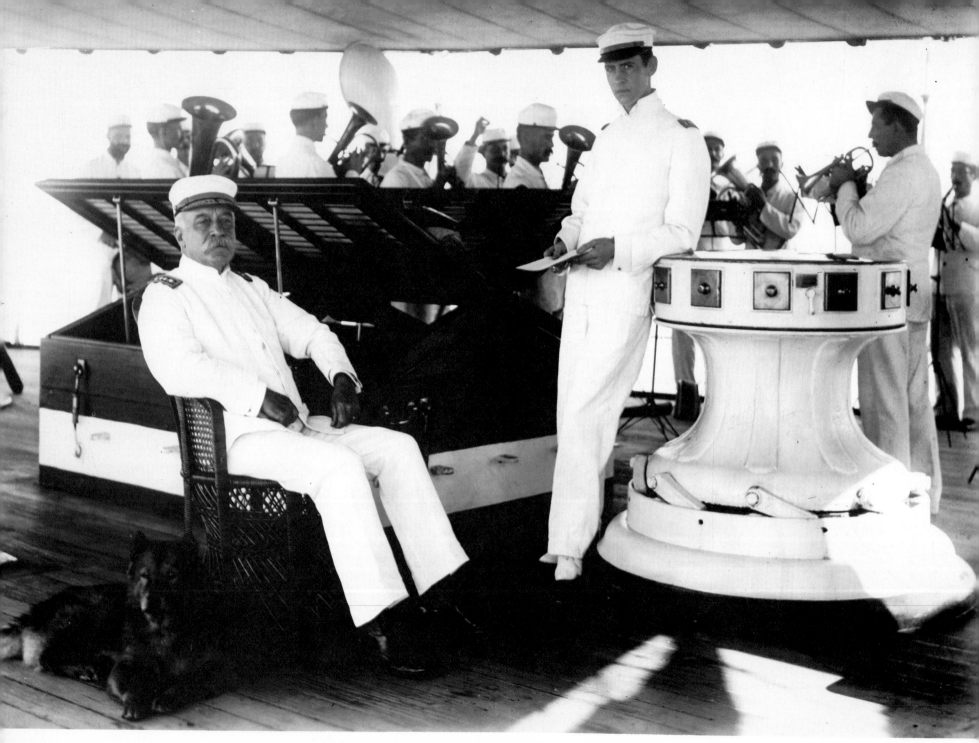

Admiral Dewey on the deck of the *Olympia* with his dog Bob

Frances Johnston in the crew's mess of the *Olympia*

Fencing on deck

An elaborate patriotic tattoo with *America* inscribed across the sailor's heart

65

Dancing sailors

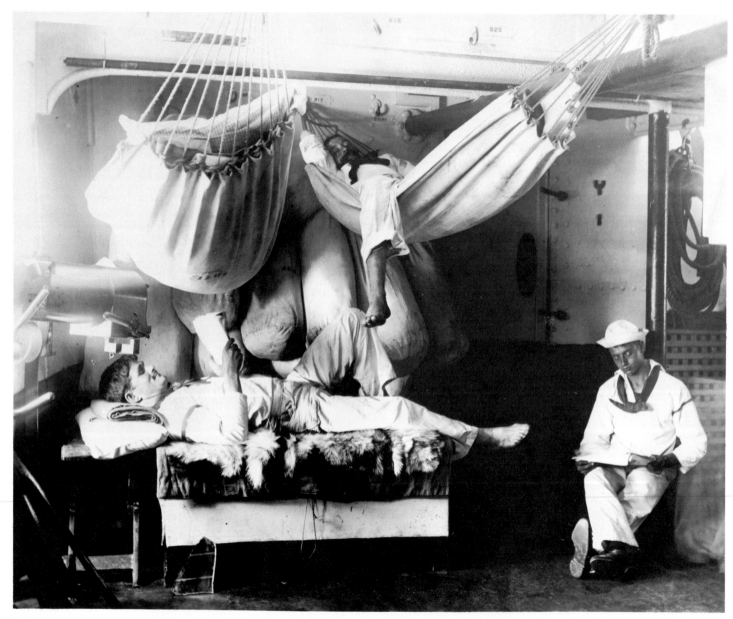

Below decks

One of Johnston's competitors, possibly J. C. Hemment

Two officers relax with one of Johnston's traveling companions beneath the *Olympia*'s big guns.

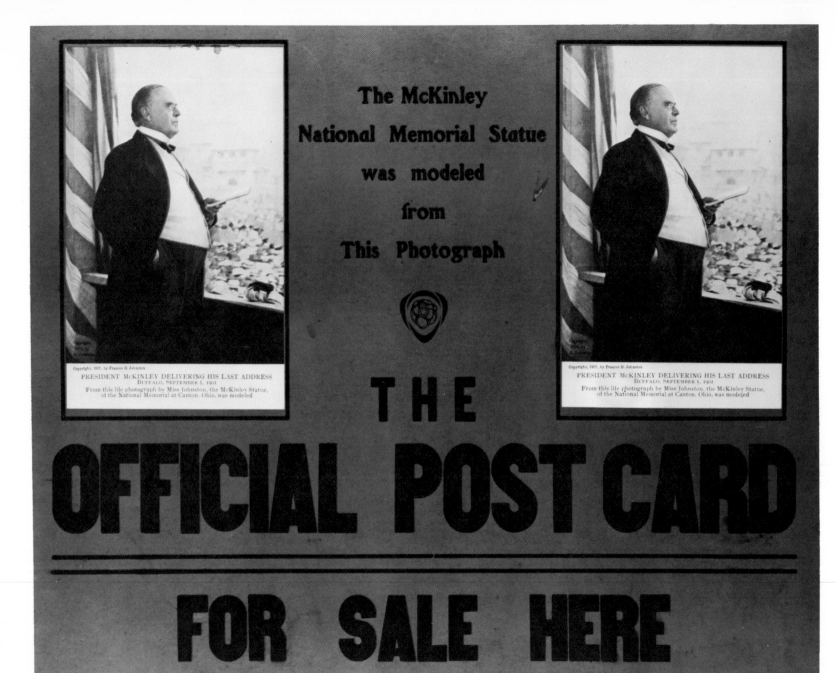

"He was always so sweet and kind and gentle," Frances remembered, "and so anxious to pose just the way you wanted him to, but always a little self-conscious before the camera, and so never at his best. But I finally caught him at the climax of a great speech, when he had wholly forgotten himself, and it proved his best portrait, and sadly enough, his last." This picture, which became known as the "Buffalo pose," was the model used to construct the statue of the President at the McKinley Monument in Canton, Ohio.

Copyright,
1901, by
F. B. Johnston

Assassination!

On 6 September 1901 President William McKinley was mortally wounded by an assassin's bullet while attending the Pan-American Exposition in Buffalo, New York. Frances Johnston had gone to the fair to photograph the president and the magnificent architecture. She had no idea that her pictures of the president would turn out to be his last.

Johnston's photographs of the president were in great demand as newspapers and magazines throughout the world clamored to publish McKinley's last pictures. While Johnston sold thousands of prints, she often failed to get the royalties she sought, and after several years she abandoned her rights to the pictures because she was weary of the business problems that resulted from such popular photographs.

Milking every ounce of dramatic effect from the pictures, each of several photographs was billed as McKinley's "last." When George Eastman discovered that Johnston had used a Number 4 Bulls-Eye Special Kodak for the McKinley pictures, he considered launching an advertising campaign to stress that she had used standard Kodak equipment.

69

President and Mrs. McKinley with Exposition president John G. Milburn touring the Pan American Exposition grounds on 5 September 1901.

Addressing the Exposition, 5 September 1901

The "last posed photograph" of President McKinley, in the Government Building on 5 September 1901. *Left to right:* Mrs. John Miller Horton, Chairwoman of the Entertainment Committee of the Woman's Board of Managers; John G. Milburn; Señor Asperoz, the Mexican Ambassador; the President; George B. Cortelyou, the President's secretary; Col. John H. Bingham of the Government Board.

The "last photograph ever taken of President McKinley," with John G. Milburn *(left)* and George B. Cortelyou *(right)*. McKinley was on his way to the Temple of Music where he was fatally wounded on 6 September 1901.

In October 1907 Frances Johnston photographed President Theodore Roosevelt (*foreground*) dedicating the McKinley Monument in Canton, Ohio. Her famous "Buffalo pose" of the martyred president was now translated into stone.

Sioux Indian chiefs with William Jennings Bryan at the Pan American Exposition. *Left to right:* F. T. Cummings, General Manager of the Exposition; High Hawk; Jack Red Cloud; Blue Horse; Little Wound; William Jennings Bryan.

"That's Bryan. He was a very determined gentleman. He looks as if he were being hideously nasty to the Indians. The Indians are rather splendid."

—ALICE ROOSEVELT LONGWORTH

A rainy day at the Pan American Exposition. At the right is the Electricity Building.

COME TO THE FAIR

World's Columbian Exposition

Johnston attended other expositions that were not marred by the tragedy of assassination. In 1892 she was on hand to record the emergence of the World's Columbian Exposition in Chicago and returned in 1893 to capture the panorama. The 150 buildings were dubbed "The White City," because the main buildings were finished with a compound called "staff," plaster of paris and jute fiber, which produced a white marble effect. In addition to the exhibition buildings, there was the Midway Plaisance, consisting of villages and street scenes from different lands. Here George W. G. Ferris presented to the world his famous revolving wheel, and there were boats and other amusements. Some 170,000 people a day streamed through the displays, and before the exposition closed over 27 million people had seen it.

Construction began in July 1891. Here craftsmen prepare ornate scrollwork.

Louisiana Purchase Exposition

The Louisiana Purchase Exposition commemorated the 100th anniversary of the Louisiana Purchase, often called the greatest bargain in American history since the size of the country was more than doubled for a cost of only $15 million, or four cents an acre. Fittingly, the exposition was vast, covering over 1,142 acres in Forest Park in St. Louis. There were fifteen large buildings, the main group laid out like a fan. There was a large amount of sculpture planned by leading artists Augustus Saint-Gaudens, John Quincy Adams Ward, and Daniel Chester French. Before the gates closed in December 1904 over 19 million people had been to the fair.

85

Stretching and yawning, Second Division School

SCHOOL DAYS

Washington, D.C., Schools

In May 1899 Johnston was commissioned to prepare a series of photographs of the Washington, D.C., schools; if successful, these photographs would become part of the United States exhibit at the Paris Exposition in 1900. She had a six-week deadline, and the commission called for 350 photographs of the schools and the children. In those days this meant trucking about all the heavy photographic equipment, getting the active children to sit still for exposures that lasted from five to twenty seconds, and then developing and printing the negatives. Her energy was incredible as she covered the schools; she made 700 negatives in six weeks.

When Johnston tried to turn her successful Washington, D.C., school photographs into financial reward, however, she failed. She agreed to use the pictures in an innovative series of sixteen booklets called *The New Education Illustrated*, each one dealing with a different aspect of school curriculum. The booklets were handsomely produced but did not sell. Like many of her business ventures, this one barely made expenses. The photographs remain, however, evocative glimpses into the past. They represent Frances Johnston's work as she was nearing the pinnacle of her career as a portraitist and documentary photographer.

The exhibit in Paris was a success, and the French government awarded her the Palmes Académiques for her role in the exposition. Her series on the District schools led other institutions to seek out her talents. Hampton Institute and Tuskegee Institute, two black schools, commissioned her, and she also photographed Carlisle Indian School in Pennsylvania. Her fame in international photographic circles was enhanced more by her school series than any single thing she had done up until that time.

Johnston's documentary eye captured a typical scene of
students boarding a trolley. Her genius for detail used the
trolley windows to frame a series of miniature portraits.

90   Science class studying water vapor, Second Division School. Johnston staged an ideal classroom setting with each student intent on the lesson. The photographer overlooked, however, the two students at the board simultaneously writing the same sentence.

Boys on their mark at a Central High School boy's track meet

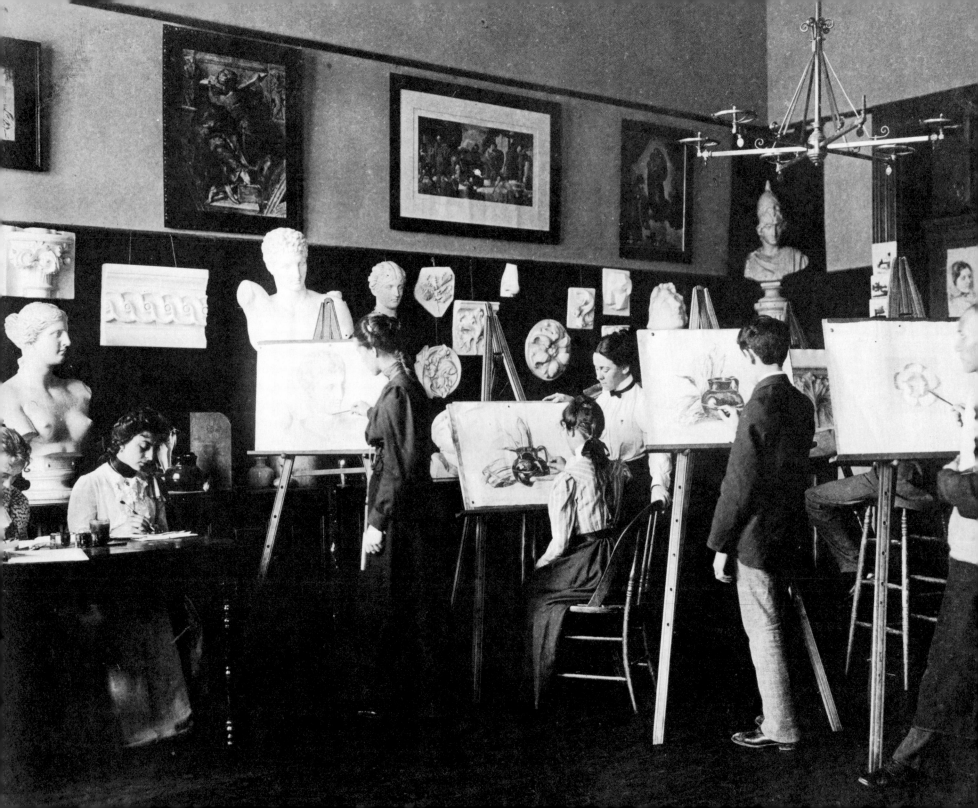

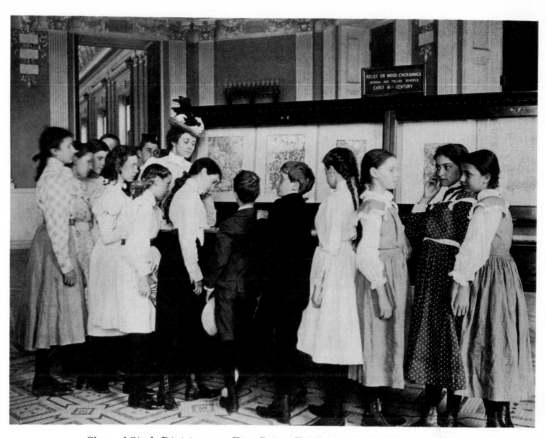

Class of Sixth Division at a Fine Prints Exhibition in the Library of Congress, Washington, D.C. Detail below.

Left: A class in painting, Central High School, Washington, D.C. Detail above.

Hampton Institute and Black Life in Rural Virginia

Winding up one of her most energetic years, Johnston went to Hampton Institute in Virginia in December 1899 to take about 150 photographs of the institute and its students. Founded by the dashing General Samuel Chapman Armstrong during Reconstruction for the education of blacks, Hampton became a model for industrial education coupled with Christian missionary zeal. Students worked their way through school in a variety of trades. Hampton's mission was to take uneducated, unskilled blacks, only recently freed from slavery, and give them the kind of education that would uplift the entire race. Ignorance and poverty were supposed to be eliminated by a rigorous regimen of hard work, practical education, and Christian piety.

Armstrong's successor as principal of Hampton, Hollis Burke Frissell, followed the same goals and wanted Johnston's photographs to show the progress that southern blacks had made under Hampton's influence. The photographs were intended for Hampton's public relations and fund

95

Hampton students sketching a boat

raising efforts. "It is part of the plan of the exhibit," wrote the editors of the *Southern Workman*, Hampton's official journal, "to contrast the new life among the Negroes and Indians with the old, and then show how Hampton has helped to produce the change."

The photographs are revealing of the Progressive Era mentality. They show social progress in visually measurable terms and assume that education can conquer a multitude of evils. In a time of bitter and overt racism, lynchings, and little opportunity for black advancement, the Hampton pictures presented the best aspiration that educators and reformers could envision at that time.

The Hampton photographs have continued to attract strong interest. In 1966, forty-four of Johnston's prints were shown at the Museum of Modern Art in New York. From this display emerged the first collection of her work published in many years, *The Hampton Album* (distributed by Doubleday & Co., Inc.). One critic for *Reporter* magazine remarked that the Hampton photographs "radiate such innocence and good hope that they make me want to cry." Some critics have raved about Johnston's technique in the Hampton photographs, comparing her to Thomas Eakins, or even "Seurat's

vibrant landscapes with roofs and tall chimneys." But the significance of the Hampton photographs, as with much of her work, was her ability to document the essence of the people and the institution. Today a viewer might find the pictures too stiff and formal or perhaps too unrealistic, but for Frances Johnston and her contemporaries her photographs captured much that could be said about the progress of a race up from slavery as well as visually presenting a vivid statement on the nature of industrial education and its goals. In terms of educational history, the Hampton studies represent a poignant view of the aspirations of the Progressive Era.

Students at work on the stairway of the treasurer's residence. The most intriguing of the Hampton photographs, this carefully composed still-life led poet Josephine Miles to write: "Down from another planet they have settled to mend The Hampton Institute banisters. They wear bow ties and braces. The flutings they polish with a polished hand."

In addition to blacks, part of the Hampton student body was composed of Indians. While Hampton-trained Indians were encouraged to cut their hair, give up tribal customs, and dress in military uniforms, in this photograph students study American history by observing a classmate in full tribal costume.

To show the contrast in the lives of southern blacks as a before-and-after sequence, Johnston traveled around the Virginia countryside and photographed poor black families and their surroundings and later juxtaposed some of these studies with the relatively prosperous Hampton graduates. The message was clear: Upward mobility and prosperity depended on industrial education and Christian piety of the Hampton type.

While Johnston's studies of black life in rural Virginia were designed primarily to contrast with the image of success at Hampton, she made many photographs that were not used in the Hampton series. These pictures stand on their own as a fine study of the countryside's fecundity —melons, hogs, syrup, wash pots, and proud but poor black families.

108

Captain Richard Henry Pratt at Carlisle Indian School, 1900

Carlisle Indian School

After the Washington schools and the Hampton Institute photographs, Johnston turned to the Carlisle Indian School in Pennsylvania. Richard Henry Pratt, a captain in the United States Army, had taken some captive Indians to Hampton in 1878 and helped to formulate a program to "civilize" them. From this experience sprang the idea of Carlisle, founded in 1879. Pratt convinced the federal government of the necessity of educating Indians, and he took one hundred twenty-nine of them to Carlisle in 1879 to begin a school in deserted army barracks. By 1904 more than twelve hundred Indian students were attending the school.

Indians in the Carlisle infirmary

Indian students debating "the Negro question." "Resolved: That the
Negroes of the South should not be denied the right [of] citizenship."

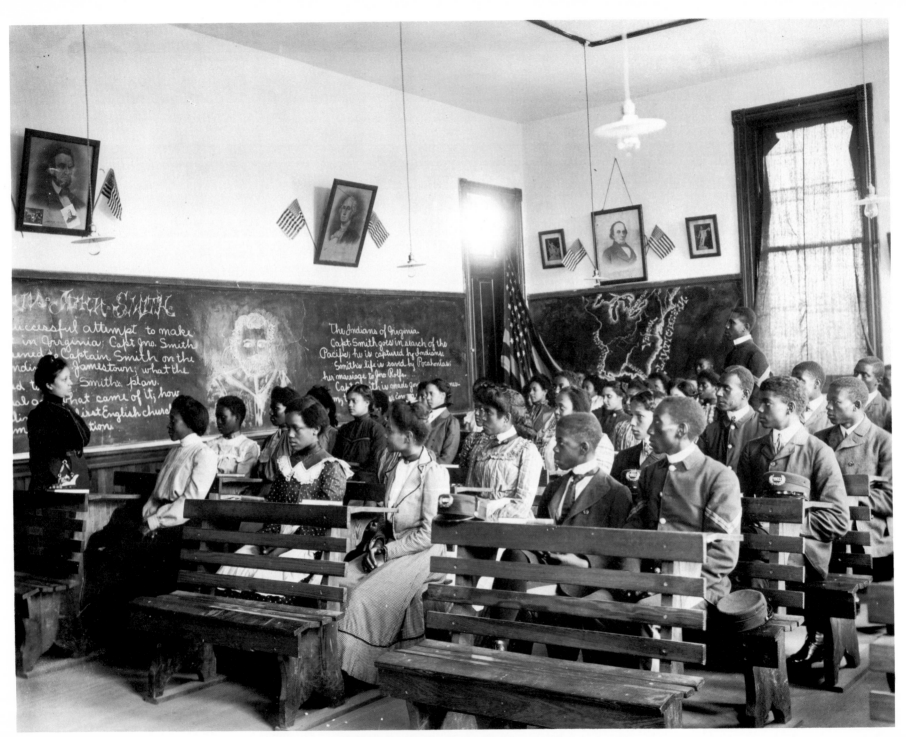

Students in a history class at Tuskegee, 1902

Tuskegee Institute

In November 1902 Johnston traveled to Tuskegee, Alabama, to take photographs of Booker T. Washington and Tuskegee Institute, which Washington had established in 1881. Washington had been educated at Hampton Institute, and there was a close relationship between the industrial programs of the two schools. In 1901 Washington's autobiography *Up from Slavery* had been published, and his fame, already established by his Atlanta speech in 1895, had increased. He spent much of each year in the North, raising funds and cultivating white philanthropists. Only a year before Johnston arrived on campus, Washington had dined at the White House with President Roosevelt, the first black man to do so, much to the dismay and anguish of white southerners. In 1906 Johnston made another trip to Alabama to study Tuskegee, but the later trip was undoubtedly a bit routine after her unusual experience in 1902.

Johnston photographed Washington, his staff, and the students at work and at their studies. Washington's message to the world was that blacks could build and manage their own institution by self-help and hard work, and Frances Johnston sought to capture this idea. She took hundreds of photographs of Tuskegee, but part of the success story of Booker T. Washington was his ability to spread his idea of industrial education, and throughout Alabama there emerged "little Tuskegees." Like missionaries, students set out to copy the master and spread literacy and Washington's gospel of hard work. One of these schools was the Ramer Colored Industrial School, and Frances decided that she would make the trip to Ramer to take photographs. The fact that she would be arriving after dark and in the company of black men did not bother her at all, for she had traveled through Europe and America and had never experienced trouble. On the same train rode George Washington Carver, who was to become famous for his work with the peanut, and who, at this time, was head of the agricultural department at Tuskegee Institute. As Carver wrote to Washington about what happened at Ramer, he had "the most frightful experience of my life there and for one day and night it was a very serious question indeed as to whether I would return to Tuskegee alive or not."

When the train arrived at the Ramer station, Nelson E. Henry, a Tuskegee graduate and principal of the school, met Johnston. He put her things into his buggy and went off into the night heading for his residence several miles out in the country. When Frances realized the length of the trip, she insisted that she be driven back to town to spend the night in a hotel. By the time she returned it was eleven o'clock and "respectable" people had gone to bed. There was no one in the streets but Postmaster George Turnipseed's son and a "desperado" named Armes. Both took offense at what they had witnessed. A white woman had been driven into the country only to return an hour later, seeking a room in the white hotel. Armes, who had allegedly run off a white school teacher several months before, drew his gun and fired three wild shots at Henry, while Carver helped Frances escape to the next town. Carver had high praise for Johnston. "I might say that she is the pluckiest woman I ever saw. She was not afraid for herself but shed bitter tears for Mr. Henry and for the school which is in all probability broken up."

Despite attempts by some of Booker T. Washington's staff and friends to calm the Ramer whites

and persuade Henry to return, the school's existence ended. Such was the nature of Alabama racism in 1902. Henry later opened a similar school in China, Alabama, and by 1912 had four teachers and ninety-six pupils. But Johnston had been thoroughly aroused by the incident. She threatened a suit against Turnipseed and Armes and went to Montgomery to see the governor, threatening to bring the power of her friend President Theodore Roosevelt down on tiny Ramer. She at least wanted Postmaster Turnipseed fired from his position.

The storm blew over, however, and the Ramer incident did not discourage Frances from continuing her work. Instead of photographing the Ramer Colored Industrial School, she went to similar schools at Snow Hill and at Mt. Meigs and photographed them. She also traveled about the countryside capturing typical scenes of black life. As her first trip was nearing its end, Emmett J. Scott, Booker T. Washington's private secretary, wrote, "She has blue prints of all the pictures she has taken here and they are far and away beyond anything of the kind we have ever had made. I am sure you will be greatly pleased with them." And after the trip in 1906 George Washington Carver wrote her that he had received the photographs and "I am well pleased with the work."

In August 1903 a number of the photographs appeared in *World's Work* in an article by Washington, "The Successful Training of the Negro." Instead of the before and after theme of the Hampton Institute work, Washington stressed the role of Tuskegee as a growing father institution for other schools. Tuskegee grew by the sweat of its own students, and they, having learned the lessons of industrial education, went out into the world to teach or to ply their trade. Education, even in those desperate days of lynching, peonage, and Jim Crow, was supposed to pave the way to respectability. But the unpublicized Ramer incident revealed the grim side of southern life even as the Tuskegee photographs illustrated the bright side.

Booker T. Washington, 1906

Booker T. Washington, 1906

Booker T. Washington, Jr. (1887–1945) was sometimes an embarrassment to his father because he took school-work lightly and preferred to spend his time with his motorcycle. But he later settled down, graduated from Fisk University, and eventually moved to Los Angeles, where he was a successful real estate broker. This photograph was taken in 1906 when Booker was nineteen years old.

Washington's success depended on his ability to tap the wealth of prominent white philanthropists. This photograph was taken during Tuskegee's twenty-fifth anniversary celebration in 1906. *Left to right:* Robert C. Ogden, William Howard Taft, Booker T. Washington, Andrew Carnegie.

Tuskegee faculty council, November 1902. *Top row, left to right:* Robert R. Taylor, R. M. Attwell, Julius B. Ramsey, Chaplain Edgar J. Penny, M. T. Driver, William Maberry, George Washington Carver. *Bottom row, left to right:* Jane E. Clark, Emmett J. Scott, Booker T. Washington, Warren Logan, John H. Washington.

Students whitewashing a fence at
Tuskegee Institute, 1902

Students cultivating onions, 1906

Woodwork shop, 1906

Millinery class, 1906

Students at Snow Hill Institute in 1902. Snow Hill was one of several "little Tuskegees" that sprang up because of the influence of Booker T. Washington's school.

In the collard patch near Snow Hill, 1902

Picking the school's cotton crop at Mt. Meigs Institute in Alabama, 1902. The proceeds from the sale of cotton helped defray the school's expenses.

Cotton being suctioned into a gin near Tuskegee, Alabama in 1902. The word "Pearline" on the wagon was the name of a nationally advertised laundry detergent.

TWO NATURAL WONDERS

Mammoth Cave by Flashlight

Intrigued by underground photography, Johnston decided to visit Mammoth Cave in Kentucky in 1892. She and her female companions donned the bloomer outfit provided by the cave managers and "were soon reveling in the luxury of unimpeded movement." She thoroughly enjoyed William Garvin, the black guide, who had a practiced talk ready as they wound their way through the different parts of the cave. Her description of the descent into the cave is reminiscent of J. R. R. Tolkien describing a fantasy world. "Pursuing our way carefully down the mossy stairway, and following a well-worn path, we feel, submerged in the dim twilight, like a small horde of vandals stealthily invading the magic realms and treasure-houses of the gnomes and pixies."

Though her photographs were much more successful than her earlier coal mine shots, she revealed nothing about her technique. "As to the difficulties, disasters, but ultimate triumph of the photographic campaign, when I sought to vanquish the arch-enemy darkness with flashpowder, it is too long a story." *Demorest's* paid her $250 for the story, the same she received for the coal mine photographs.

Frances Johnston at the mouth of Mammoth Cave

Johnston observed that there was "no settlement near the cave—no habitation, in fact, except the great rambling hotel—which, little by little, has been evolved from the original log cabin."

On the Echo River in Mammoth Cave in 1891

Even in 1892 there were the usual reminders left by tourists. In Mammoth Cave the visitor might occasionally find calling cards tucked away in corners, but the most popular ways to make contributions to posterity were either to write one's name on the ceiling or to erect a cairn, a rock pile. "Found in all the well-traveled avenues of the cave, these cairns number several hundred, and frequently reach to the ceiling. They have been erected by tourists, as memorials to cities, states, countries, famous men and women, societies, and colleges."

By the time she visited the cave's bridal chamber, nine couples had been wed there and Johnston recorded the legend "of the pioneer subterranean bride, who, having pledged her mother that she would '*never marry a man on the face of the earth*,' here fulfilled the letter, if not the spirit, of her vow, by an underground wedding."

Yellowstone by Stagecoach

Yellowstone, wonderland of pulsing fountains, hot rivers, cascading waterfalls, and bears. Before tourists claimed the park, this land was a dividing line among different Indian tribes of the area, most tribes regarding it as sacred ground. Lewis and Clark heard only superficial accounts of the area on their famous journey, but John Colter trapped in the area in 1806, and little by little the world learned of Yellowstone.

Eventually the area was duly explored, and in 1872 Congress established Yellowstone as a National Park. Interest in the area boomed, and even President Chester Arthur visited the park in 1883. Roads were carved out to accommodate the tourists, but until 1915 travel was by horseback and stagecoach.

Johnston's photographs, probably taken in 1903, show Yellowstone in its evolving state; the roads were narrow, the tourists few. These photographs show the park in a purity that has disappeared beneath the tramping of millions of tourists. Unfortunately, Frances Johnston left no written account of her journey to Yellowstone other than brief descriptive notes hastily scrawled on the back of some of her prints.

Fording the Firehole River at Yellowstone National Park

Frances Johnston at Yellowstone National Park

Tourists examining geysers at Yellowstone

Mule skinner at Yellowstone

Joe Knowles, Johnston's driver at
Yellowstone National Park

Early Yellowstone traffic jam

Lower Falls of the Yellowstone

AN AMERICAN GALLERY

142

AN AMERICAN GALLERY

The Twinkle of his Eye

Although Frances Johnston rarely left a written description of her portrait work, she did write a vivid account of her encounter with Joel Chandler Harris.

"Photograph Joel Chandler Harris!" Frances's friends were incredulous. Harris, they revealed, was so shy that at a banquet in his honor he failed to appear. It seemed that the author of Uncle Remus and Br'er Rabbit stories liked the privacy of his own briar patch, his "Snap-Bean Farm," which Johnston described as "low, rambling, of many gables, and surrounded by ample and shady verandas." She set off to Atlanta in April 1905 with letters of introduction. "The novelty of finding in a favorite author a man who really did not want to be photographed lent zest to the pursuit," she remembered.

"I found him a man of medium height and comfortably rounded outlines, rather slow and hesitant in his movements, but much younger in appearance than his actual years seemed to justify."

"His face was round and ruddy and whole-

143

somely freckled like a country boy's," Johnston continued, "and all his wonderful gifts of understanding, of sympathy, of humour, of pathos and of tenderness were held in his eyes—deep set, very wide apart and of the bluest blue ever. A black sombrero-shaped hat was tilted at a characteristic angle on the back of his very blond head; a close-cropped, sandy mustache covered a full lipped, mobile, sensitive mouth which had a whimsical twist at one corner; but his most vital characteristic was the illuminating twinkle of his eye."

She found him in comfortable clothes, but he was a bit excited, she thought, "his manner being an appealing mixture of gentleness, good humor and panic." She managed to ease his panic and take his mind off posing. Evidently this was her secret in portrait photography; she could ease the "stiff pose and wooden expression" which most people assumed when a camera was near. She was satisfied when she left that Harris had revealed his twinkle for her camera. "It was an experience that I will never forget and will always treasure," she remembered, "for it is permitted to very few to meet the embodiment of an ideal on such intimate terms and come away with it strengthened and enriched a hundredfold."

Harris was elated with the photographs. "I wish I could adequately thank you for the photographs. I wish I could tell you word for word and thought for thought how very much I appreciate your kindness in the matter, and how keen my delight in them is! Because they are the first real photographs of myself that I have ever seen and because, too, I have now found out for the first time what you meant by the twinkle. The twinkle seems to be me, myself, after all, and I have been going on all these years, not knowing what was missing from the photographs I had taken by people who knew nothing about the twinkle. I realize now that real photography is one of the arts. Mrs. Harris is wildly enthusiastic about them. She declares that your portraits represent me as she sees me."

And the photograph of Harris with his twinkle would represent him as the world would remember him. This photograph came to grace the stationery of Harris's *Uncle Remus' Home Magazine*. It also was used for the Harris commemorative postage stamp issued in 1948, and it was the dust jacket photograph for Robert L. Wiggins, *The Life of Joel Chandler Harris*.

Susan B. Anthony

The photographs of Susan Brownell Anthony are perhaps the most interesting study Johnston did of an American woman. Born in Massachusetts in 1820, Anthony became one of the most outstanding Americans of the nineteenth century. After a brief teaching career she became interested in reform, especially women's rights. By the 1850s she attracted other notable American women to her cause —Amelia Bloomer, Lucretia Mott, Lucy Stone, and Elizabeth Cady Stanton. Her causes included abolition, temperance, and voting rights for blacks and women, but especially equal rights for women. When Johnston photographed her in 1900, Anthony was eighty years old, still alert, graceful, determined, and exuding the dignity that had carried her through many crusades. Anthony had slight strabismus (discoordination of the eyes) and was walleyed. Because of this she wanted to be photographed in profile, but Johnston did manage to persuade her to be posed full front. These photographs later appeared on the Anthony Calendar, a forerunner of the women's liberation calendar. A section of the calendar is reproduced on the following page.

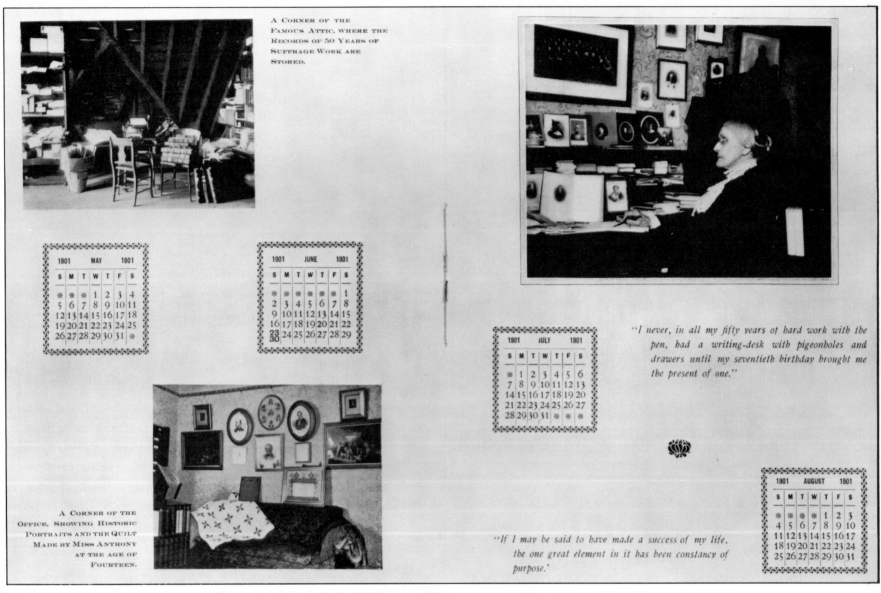

A CORNER OF THE
FAMOUS ATTIC, WHERE THE
RECORDS OF 50 YEARS OF
SUFFRAGE WORK ARE
STORED.

1901	MAY	1901

S	M	T	W	T	F	S
✳	✳	1	2	3	4
5	6	7	8	9	10	11
12	13	14	15	16	17	18
19	20	21	22	23	24	25
26	27	28	29	30	31	✳

1901	JUNE	1901

S	M	T	W	T	F	S
✳	✳	✳	✳	✳	1
2	3	4	5	6	7	8
9	10	11	12	13	14	15
16	17	18	19	20	21	22
23 30	24	25	26	27	28	29

1901	JULY	1901

S	M	T	W	T	F	S
✳	1	2	3	4	5	6
7	8	9	10	11	12	13
14	15	16	17	18	19	20
21	22	23	24	25	26	27
28	29	30	31	✳	✳	✳

"I never, in all my fifty years of hard work with the pen, had a writing-desk with pigeonholes and drawers until my seventieth birthday brought me the present of one."

A CORNER OF THE
OFFICE, SHOWING HISTORIC
PORTRAITS AND THE QUILT
MADE BY MISS ANTHONY
AT THE AGE OF
FOURTEEN.

1901	AUGUST	1901

S	M	T	W	T	F	S
✳	✳	✳	✳	1	2	3
4	5	6	7	8	9	10
11	12	13	14	15	16	17
18	19	20	21	22	23	24
25	26	27	28	29	30	31

"If I may be said to have made a success of my life, the one great element in it has been constancy of purpose.'

A page from the 1901 Susan B. Anthony Calendar

Susan B. Anthony in her study

The First Family

In 1902 Johnston persuaded Theodore Roosevelt to allow her to photograph his children. She remembered that it was the president's wish that his children be spared the usual attention that White House children received from the press, so that they could grow up unspoiled. It was impossible, of course, to hide beautiful Alice Roosevelt.

"I was sent to the White House one day to get pictures of the four children for Jacob Riis," Johnston explained, "with the president's permission, and his signature on an impressive document." Riis, a well-known journalist and photographer, was a long-time friend of the president.

Johnston's first problem was finding the children. "Miss Alice, as Mrs. Longworth was then, finally located them for me under their beds," she recalled. The photograph of Teddy, Jr., was taken in the conservatory, then located at the west front of the White House. At another time, she photographed the president and his wife.

President and Mrs. Roosevelt, 18 December 1902

"Isn't this picture pure rapture?
What an incredible dress; it had a
sort of bib in front. I know that I
must look as funny here as some
of you will if you stay around as
long as I have. You seldom get
as good a laugh as when you are
looking at old photographs of
yourself."
—ALICE ROOSEVELT LONGWORTH

Alice Roosevelt in the White House
conservatory, 18 December 1902

Alice Roosevelt on horseback

"The horse was a sturdy object from Fort Myer. They sent over a horse and one got on it. That horrible horse. I like this photograph, though; terribly funny and so of the epoch." —ALICE ROOSEVELT LONGWORTH

Alice Roosevelt in riding clothes

Quentin Roosevelt and a playmate,
Rosewell Flower Pinckney

Quentin and Kermit Roosevelt with the White House police, 1902

"I'll always remember this photograph. We never had the Secret Service following us around. My stepmother and a friend would go downtown to shop and they were never followed. The police did watch over the children to make sure they didn't make monkeys of themselves. Even after McKinley was shot, in September of 1901, and we moved into the White House, the Security Police consisted of only these five men. (At least they were the only ones I ever saw.) It's incredible to see what the White House has turned into in the last fifty years. They have so many Secret Service cars and people acting as guards. It wasn't like that when we were in the White House."

—ALICE ROOSEVELT LONGWORTH

153

Theodore Roosevelt. The hero of San Juan Hill wanted posterity to remember him at his best; his new Brooks Brothers uniform had arrived only fifteen minutes before Johnston took these photographs. She had journeyed to Montauk Point, Long Island, in August 1898 to record the return from Cuba of the glamorous Rough Riders, who were waiting for their separation from the army. Johnston was to have a long and fruitful photographic relationship with Roosevelt and his family.

Theodore Roosevelt and the Rough Riders, 1898

Theodore Roosevelt, Jr., with his parrot Eli in the White House conservatory, 18 December 1902

American Portraits

Alexander Graham Bell (1847–1922), a scientist, inventor, and teacher of the deaf, he is best known for his invention of the telephone, which was patented in 1876. Bell was president of the National Geographic Society from 1896 to 1904. As a final tribute to Bell at the time of his burial, all telephone service on the North American continent was momentarily halted.

Ida Saxton McKinley, a former cashier in her father's bank in Canton, Ohio, married William McKinley in 1871. A series of personal tragedies resulting in the death of her four-year-old child and then another child who died in infancy, plus the loss of her mother, caused a nervous disorder that left her an invalid for the rest of her life. Despite her handicap she managed the duties of First Lady.

"This picture of Mrs. McKinley shows the kind of enormous, upholstered clothing that was worn at the time. Apparently, she was apt to have little fits or spasms. She always sat next to the President and when she'd have her little fit, he would put a napkin over her face until the spasm was over. I'm not being inventive; I'm being accurate."
—ALICE ROOSEVELT LONGWORTH

President William McKinley, 1898

"When McKinley was shot I was seventeen. I came out, as we did in those days, and had a party, so I must have been seventeen. He was shot in September and we moved into the White House."

—ALICE ROOSEVELT LONGWORTH

Jacob August Riis (1849–1914). An immigrant from Denmark, he began his journalistic career in America as a police reporter in New York City. Riis used his camera and pen to expose the evils of poverty in big-city slums in his classic study, *How the Other Half Lives* (1890). Later he wrote a popular autobiography, *The Making of an American* (1901).

Mark Twain (1835–1910). The famous American humorist and author was photographed in December 1906. A few years later, in 1909, he predicted, in characteristic Twain fashion, the end of his own life. "I came in with Halley's Comet in 1835. It is coming again next year, and I expect to go out with it. It will be the greatest disappointment of my life if I don't go out with Halley's Comet. The Almighty has said, no doubt: 'Now here are these two unaccountable freaks; they came in together, they must go out together.'"

Jane E. Clark was dean of the
women's department at Tuskegee
Institute from 1902 to 1906.

Andrew Carnegie (1835–1919). This portrait of the famous steel magnate and philanthropist was taken in April 1905. Carnegie once said of "instantaneous photography" that it was "a great thing ... one has not the time to look his very worst, as sitters usually contrive to do."

Phoebe Apperson Hearst (1842–1919), the mother of newspaper magnate William Randolph Hearst, was a noted philanthropist of her day.

George Washington Carver (1864–1943) was born in slavery in Missouri and rose to be a distinguished agricultural scientist. Frances Johnston photographed Carver in 1906 when she visited Tuskegee Institute. Carver often wore a boutonniere of weeds or unusual flowers and, when asked why he had such weeds in his lapel, would take delight in explaining their many uses.

Left to right: Booker T. Washington; Booker T. Washington, Jr.; E. Davidson Washington; 1906

Margaret James Murray Washington (1861?–1925), Booker T. Washington's third wife, was "Lady Principal" and later dean of women at Tuskegee Institute. She was also a national leader in the black women's club movement.

Mrs. John Phillip Sousa and daughters, March 1904

John Phillip Sousa (1854–1932), the "March King," devoted his life to music, beginning as a music teacher at age fifteen. He was United States Marine Corps band leader from 1880 to 1892 before launching his own famous Sousa's Band.

Helen Hay (Mrs. Payne Whitney) was the daughter of Secretary of State John Hay. She was a poet and also wrote children's stories. Typical of her poems are the following lines from "The Price" in *Gypsy Verses* (1907):

We are so tired of merely being human,
Loving or loved, the sweet imperfect woman,
Masters, you know not what your lips have
        missed,
On the rose mouths you keep but to be kissed.

John Milton Hay (1838–1905) was United States Secretary of State from 1898 to 1905. In his earlier careers he was a poet, journalist, and historian. Once private secretary to Abraham Lincoln, Hay collaborated with John G. Nicolay in a ten-volume study of Lincoln.

Richard Hovey (1864–1900) was a poet whose untimely death brought a promising career to an end. In his last poem he wrote:

At last, O death,
Not with the sick-room fever and weary heart
And slow subsistence of diminished breath—
But strong and free
With the great tumult of the living sea . . .

Julia Marlowe was an actress who began her career at the age of nine. She became a distinguished Shakespearean actress noted especially for her role as Juliet. She managed a Shakespearean company with her first husband, Robert Taber, until his death in 1904. In 1911 she married another leading man, Edward Hugh Sothern. At the Columbia Exposition in 1893 she spoke on the importance of women in the theatre and reminded her audience of the problems women had in the 1600s when women's roles were played by men. She thought it absurd that a role like Juliet should be played by a male actor. Perhaps this photograph was taken in 1898 when Marlowe appeared in Washington, D.C., in *The Countess of Valeska*, one of her most successful roles.

General Leonard Wood (1860–1927) was a civilian trained M.D. who rose to become one of the outstanding soldiers of his time. An Indian fighter in the 1880s and Commander of the Rough Riders during the Spanish-American War, he became military governor of Cuba and later reorganized the United States Army as chief of staff. He was governor general of the Philippines from 1921 to 1927.

Benjamin Ryan Tillman (1847–1918). Known as "Pitchfork Ben," Tillman was the United States Senator from South Carolina from 1895 to 1918. Tillman had a glass eye which Johnston masked by careful use of lighting.

Albert Jeremiah Beveridge (1862–1927). As a boy Beveridge worked on a farm and on railroads and at age fifteen was a teamster for a logging camp. He eventually acquired an education and became a lawyer and United States Senator from Indiana (1899–1911). He was also a noted author and historian. Johnston photographed him in 1905, midway through his two terms in the Senate.

"This must be Albert Jeremiah Beveridge. He looks very upstanding in his tight collar. He was a senator who was full of noble thoughts and not unwilling to voice them."
—ALICE ROOSEVELT LONGWORTH

Jane Cowl (1883–1950), an actress, posed for Johnston in 1908. Considered one of the most beautiful women of the American stage, she often complained that once a stage career was launched, beauty became a hindrance rather than an advantage. In addition to acting she wrote several successful plays. In the last year of her life she played a few minor roles in Hollywood films.

Gifford Pinchot (1865–1946), a champion of conservation, was the first professional forester in America. In 1903 he began a thirty-year career as professor of forestry at Yale. He also served two terms as governor of Pennsylvania from 1923 to 1927, and from 1931 to 1935.

Taken about 1900, this interpretive portrait entitled "The Critic" was described by one reviewer in *Photo Era Magazine* as Johnston "at her best from the purely artistic standpoint."

Neith Boyce Hapgood, a novelist and journalist, was married in 1899 to another author, Hutchins Hapgood.